Bonolo
and
the Peach Tree

written by
Njabulo S. Ndebele
illustrations by
James Ransome

HARCOURT BRACE & COMPANY
Orlando   Atlanta   Austin   Boston   San Francisco   Chicago   Dallas   New York
Toronto   London

Bonolo
and
the Peach Tree

written by
Njabulo S. Ndebele
illustrations by
James Ransome

Illustrations by James Ransome
Illustrations copyright © 1994 by Harcourt Brace & Company

This edition is published by special arrangement with Ravan Press (Pty) Ltd.

Grateful acknowledgment is made to Ravan Press (Pty) Ltd., P. O. Box
31134, Braamfontein, 2017 Johannesburg, South Africa, for permission
to reprint *Bonolo and the Peach Tree* by Njabulo S. Ndebele. Originally
published in South Africa by Ravan Press (Pty) Ltd. © 1992 by Njabulo
S. Ndebele.

Printed in the United States of America

ISBN 0-15-302192-6

1 2 3 4 5 6 7 8 9 10   011   97 96 95 94 93

Contents

1

A Boy of Strange Ways

THE VILLAGE of Iketsetse is one of the most beautiful in Lesotho. It lies in a big valley deep in the mountains of the district of Mokhotlong. The people of Iketsetse settled there many years ago and built their village of houses, shops, market-places, schools, churches, the hospital, the post office, the community hall, the saw mills and pulp-making factory, and the small electricity station. Way beyond were corn and wheat and sorghum fields that stretched far into the distance, merging with the evergreen forest that covered the surrounding mountains.

Ever since they settled in that valley, the people of Iketsetse have worked tirelessly, forever thinking of new ways of making their village even more beautiful.

In that village there also lived Bonolo, a boy of strange ways. To Bonolo, everything in his village seemed to have always been there, as if one morning, in some distant past, the sun had risen, and the people of Iketsetse had woken up in the wilderness to find themselves in a new village. To Bonolo, his village could not have been built with human hands.

Bonolo lived with his mother and father, 'Mabonolo and Rabonolo. 'Mabonolo, his mother, was a weaver; Rabonolo, a carpenter. From the time he learned to walk, Bonolo loved nothing more than to follow his father into the carpentry shop. Once there, he would wedge himself into a corner, and watch his father making furniture.

First, Rabonolo made designs on a large sheet of white paper. Then, after sticking the pencil behind his ear, he would walk over to the piles of wood on the other side of the shop, where he inspected the wood carefully until he finally selected what he needed. Then, using saws of many shapes and sizes, he would cut the wood into many different pieces. These he would smooth carefully with a plane, and then begin to shape them according to his designs, or make joints, chipping at the pieces of wood ever so delicately with various chisels and mallets. At that point, he would put aside the wood and his tools for a moment, and go outside to make a fire to boil a pot of glue. And finally, after many hours of work, came the moment of wonder! This was the moment Bonolo waited for, as if nothing else had happened until then.

As Rabonolo joined this piece of wood with that piece of wood, this next piece of wood with that other piece of wood, a miracle beyond description slowly took shape before Bonolo's eyes. It was like the rising of the full moon in the early evening. You can see it coming up slowly from behind the mountains, a glowing red little piece of a circle, becoming larger and larger as it rises, until it turns finally into a huge shining silver circle.

In that same way, a chair, or a table, or a window-frame, or a cabinet, slowly emerged out of the hands of Rabonolo. What had not been there before gradually appeared before Bonolo's eyes. And each time he saw this wonder, his joy would spread across his face.

There was one more moment that Bonolo waited for. It was the arrival of his father's customers coming to fetch their orders.

'Father of Bonolo,' they would invariably exclaim, 'what a wonderful pair of hands you've got!'

'It is your happiness that matters,' Rabonolo would say, looking embarrassed. 'Come, let me show you.' Rabonolo would explain how that wonderful piece of furniture came to be standing there before them.

Out of sheer happiness, some of the customers would turn towards Bonolo and lift him up into their arms. 'And when are you going to make us your furniture?' they asked.

And others with them would answer, 'With time, with time!'

Rabonolo did not fail to notice the glow of enchantment on his son's face. This pleased him no end, for indeed he thought that perhaps one day Bonolo would himself become a carpenter. Certainly, it seemed his thoughts were answered when one day Rabonolo heard some of Bonolo's first words as the boy learned to speak, much earlier than many other children: 'pencil,' 'wood,' 'fire,' 'glue,' 'table,' 'chair,' and several other words that carpenters use.

Well before Bonolo could speak in sentences, Rabonolo would pick him up under the armpits, throw him into the air, only to catch him again and throw him up once more, all the while saying:

'This little man will be like his father
This little man will be a carpenter.
This little man will be like his father,
This little man will be a carpenter.'

Then one day, closing his eyes, his mind enchanted by the ease with which his father's hands brought things out into the world, Bonolo uttered his first sentence:

'I will be a carpenter,' he said.

2

In the Carpentry Shop

ALTHOUGH RABONOLO was pleased that his son was fascinated by carpentry, he was uneasy about Bonolo's spending so much time alone without the company of his age-mates. Children must be out there playing with others, thought Rabonolo. He remembered from his own days the joys of being with one's friends.

There were many neighbourhood friends for Bonolo. Most important of all was Tsepo, son of the bus driver from the next house. Tsepo never failed to ask Bonolo to come along to enjoy a day's journey as a non-paying passenger in a bus driven by his father. He would come with enticing stories about the wonders of distant places. But Bonolo always turned down his friend's invitation. He preferred to be in his father's carpentry shop. This always disappointed Tsepo, for he loved Bonolo dearly. Finally, Tsepo drifted away from Bonolo, who would not even come out to play.

'Anyway,' Rabonolo consoled himself, 'we all outgrow our habits. Bonolo will soon want the company of his friends.'

It was not long, however, before Rabonolo noticed a new development in his son's behaviour. Once Bonolo had crawled into the carpentry shop and settled in his favourite corner, he would watch his father work for a few minutes only. Then he would close his eyes and keep them closed for as long as his father was working.

'Is he sleeping?' Rabonolo wondered. His son's behaviour puzzled him. Day after day, Bonolo would come into the shop, wedge himself into his corner, and close his eyes, seemingly fast asleep.

But what his father did not know was that Bonolo was not really sleeping. He liked simply to listen to the movements of his father, guessing not only where his father was at each moment, but also from the sounds he made, what he was doing.'Now my father is drawing his designs,' Bonolo said to himself. There would be so much silence he could hear his father breathing.

He could hear the hissing sound of the pencil as it moved on the paper. He could tell when his father was erasing something. Sometimes the rubbing was so hard and strong that it made the table squeak. Sometimes, especially when the rubbing had been vigorous, there would be a swishing. sweeping sound as his father brushed clean the paper with his hand.

'Now he is choosing the wood.' There would be

the sound of pulling and mild banging of wood against wood.

'Now he is cutting the wood. From the sound of the sawing. I know the size of the wood. I can also tell the size of the saw.' And the sawing would continue until Bonolo was almost lulled to sleep, only to be awakened by the silence following the sawing.

'Now my father is hammering, chipping away with his chisels. He is making joints.' Then there would follow a long silence which was soon ended by the smell of fire, as his father prepared the glue. 'And now the fire and the glue.' Soon the shop would be full of the smell of fire, wood, and glue. Then silence.

At this point, Bonolo was always tempted to open his eyes. But it was not yet time. The silence was broken by the sound of light hammering: a little hammering here, and a little hammering there.

'Something is about to appear,' Bonolo would say to himself, excitement rising in him like water filling up a cup. 'Is it a chair, a table, a desk . . . or what? And there now, the sound of sandpaper. Whatever it is that was being made, has now been made.' And only at that moment would Bonolo open his eyes just in time to see the finished chair, or table, or desk, or whatever piece of furniture his father may have been asked to make. And Bonolo would feel such joy in him as if he himself had made that piece of furniture, working at it from beginning to end: as if it were his.

As days passed, and then weeks and months, the pictures of his father's work became clearer and clearer in Bonolo's mind. They became so clear that Bonolo began to see more clearly with his eyes closed. He began to see not only where his father was and what he was doing in the carpentry shop, but also the expression on his face, and the look of his hands and fingers.

He saw also the fine shades of colour on the wood as well as the natural designs on it. He saw the sawdust squirting out like an intermittent waterfall when his father was cutting the wood. He saw the sawdust fluttering down to settle on the floor, making mole hills that his father would unknowingly trample flat, leaving the imprint of the designs from under the soles of his boots.

Bonolo would see the bubbles of boiling glue forming and popping, forming and popping like so many eyes opening and closing. Indeed, the longer Bonolo closed his eyes, the more clearly he saw.

One day, something remarkable began to happen. As Bonolo sat there in his corner, seeing with his mind, he began to see himself wherever his father was. Slowly but firmly, he began to feel as if he were his father, a carpenter. It was he who was now making furniture. He made such furniture as he imagined had never been made before in the world. He made tables and chairs decorated with wings or butterflies, delicately glued onto the furniture in the most enchanting arrangements. He

9

made benches cushioned with ever-fresh yellow flowers of aloes. He turned wood into glass and made glass beds that blinked continuously with rainbow colors. The more furniture Bonolo made in his mind, the easier it became to make it, and the more enchanting it became.

3
Bonolo's Apprenticeship

I T WAS not long before Rabonolo noticed something else about his son. The boy was definitely growing. He had the bones of his grandfather. Tall and sturdy. Surely he was old enough now to send around the shop. After all, boys of his age in the village were now going out into the fields to take care of their father's goats, sheep, and cattle. If Bonolo could not go out to play with his friends, he could at least start helping in the carpentry shop. This habit of sitting in a corner and sleeping was not good. Something had to be done about this.

'Son!' said Rabonolo one Sunday evening just before bedtime as the family was sitting and talking after supper.

'Yes, father!' responded Bonolo.

'Come and sit here,' said Rabonolo patting his lap. Bonolo eagerly leapt onto his father's lap

12

where he was dandled up and down to his great delight. 'Yes!' said Rabonolo after a while, smiling. 'You are heavy enough. Now is the time. It is time for you to be a carpenter.'

There was silence in the room as everyone expected Bonolo's face to break into a smile. But instead, they saw a puzzled face.

'But, father,' said Bonolo. 'I *am* a carpenter!'

His parents laughed at this, thinking it was their son's way of saying: 'Yes, father, I'm going to work with you as a carpenter.'

'Good!' shouted Rabonolo as he hugged his son close to him. 'Tomorrow, my child, is the beginning of another week of work. I want it to be the beginning of something else too, something that all people treasure to the end of their lives. Tomorrow I want you to take your first step towards becoming one of the best carpenters this world has ever seen.'

As'Mabonolo looked at her son, pride shone in her face. But suddenly, Bonolo struggled free from his father's embrace, jumped down, and looked at his father with a worried face.

'But, father! I *am* a carpenter already!' Bonolo said firmly, and walked away to his bedroom. His mother and father exchanged puzzled glances and laughed. They did not know what was going on in their son's mind.

That night, Bonolo took a long time to fall asleep. He was worried. He wanted nothing more than to go on sitting in his corner with his eyes closed and doing all that wonderful work. Why did his father not choose a corner too, and just sit there and make all the world's best furniture? Why all the sweat? No. He would not go to the carpentry shop tomorrow. He *was* a carpenter, as good as any in the world.

The following morning Rabonolo got up earlier than usual, and went to the workshop. There he first cleaned up, and then began to sharpen all his chisels and saws, and selected the best wood available. Soon he was ready for the work of the day. He felt sure that when Bonolo came in through the door the boy would not only feel the newness of the day, of the week, but also the exciting freshness of that most important of all beginnings: learning how to work.

And so, once he had done all the preparations, Rabonolo expectantly looked at the door each time he thought he heard some movement. But nothing happened. Next he thought he heard a voice and he called out and asked: 'Is that you, son?' But nothing happened. And yet again, Rabonolo went to the door, and then again to the door, until it was mid-morning, but still there was no sign of Bonolo.

Finally, Rabonolo went to the door and called out: 'Bonolo!'

There was no reply. He went across to the house and looked in every room. There was no Bonolo. He went back outside and cast his eyes towards the rondavel on the other side of the yard, where his wife did her weaving. He wondered if Bonolo was there. But why would his mother not have sent him over to the workshop? Surely she knew the day's plans!

'Bonolo!' he called out once more. But once more, there was no response.

Rabonolo decided to go across to the rondavel. When he entered, he saw his wife, 'Mabonolo, working quietly at her loom, and just behind her, sitting on a mat on the floor, was Bonolo, looking so intently at his mother weaving that he did not even notice his father come in. Nor did Bonolo hear his father harshly calling his name, until his father shook him, lifting him up from the floor with his powerful hands. Only then did Bonolo seem to come out of a deep trance. Only then, also, did 'Mabonolo notice that Bonolo was in the rondavel with her. Bonolo had sneaked in while his mother was working intently at her loom.

'What are you doing here?' Rabonolo shouted at his son, and began to drag him away. 'Didn't I ask you yesterday to come to the workshop this morning?' 'Mabonolo looked at her husband. It had been a long time since she had seen him angry. 'Please,' she pleaded, 'leave him alone. He means no harm. Don't force him. Let him stay here for a while if that's what he wants to do.'

Rabonolo seemed to notice his wife for the first time when she spoke. His mind had been full of Bonolo all morning. He felt deeply pained and disappointed. 'You left him to hide here! Why didn't you send him to me?' Rabonolo was still shouting.

'I was not aware he was here,' said 'Mabonolo.

16

'You were not aware, indeed! The boy was sitting right next to you.' Then he turned towards his son. 'You!' he fiercely waved a finger at Bonolo. 'You're coming with me to the workshop, this very minute! Your days of sitting in idleness are over. I will not bring up an indolent, disgraceful child.' Then he began to drag Bonolo out of the rondavel towards the carpentry shop. And so began Bonolo's days as an apprentice. They did not last.

It did not take long for Rabonolo to realise that Bonolo could never put his mind to anything he was told to do. He could never lay his hand on anything he was told to bring. Instead, Bonolo would only dream of things that did his bidding. For example, if he was told to bring along a piece of wood, Bonolo simply stood wherever he was, closed his eyes, and tried to bring the wood to him with his mind. Not surprisingly, the wood did not obey. And since he believed that the piece of wood was actually there in his hands, Bonolo opened his eyes, stretched his arms towards his father and said: 'Father, here is the wood.'

Not surprisingly, Rabonolo saw nothing in his son's hands.

Yet again, when Bonolo was asked to bring a saw, he closed his eyes and not only did he command the saw to come to him, but he also began to cut some wood with it. Only when he had finished cutting the wood did he open his eyes, turn towards his father and say: 'Father I have already cut the wood.'

Not surprisingly, Rabonolo saw nothing but his son's empty hands.

And when Bonolo was asked to make fire to boil the glue, he became even more diligent. He closed his eyes and, with the hands of his mind, not only made the fire, but also mixed the glue, boiled it, and then, carried away by the ease of it all, Bonolo began to do much more than his father had asked. He began to join pieces of wood together until, all by himself, he had assembled a piece of furniture. Then he opened his eyes, turned towards his father and said: 'At last, father, I have finished. Now, this chair can be sold.'

Not surprisingly, Rabonolo saw no new chair in the workshop.

At first, Rabonolo thought there was going to be much fun in the carpentry shop: his son had a great sense of humour. But soon he changed his mind. Was the boy playing the fool, making fun of his father? No, it couldn't be. Was it that the boy, perhaps, was still too young to work? But then, boys of his age were out there in the fields doing useful work, helping their families to live. Rabonolo wondered. Whatever Rabonolo thought about his son, one thing was clear, Bonolo could not continue working in the workshop.

'Son,' Rabonolo said at last, 'perhaps you should go to your mother's rondavel, and have a little change.' And so, Bonolo went to his mother's rondavel, where a new world began for him.

4

The Marvellous Weaver

BONOLO BEGAN to watch his mother at work. He watched with the same interest with which he had watched his father at work. What did he see now?

Bonolo watched his mother sorting raw mohair that she had taken out from bales and bales of mohair in the store room. He noticed how she washed the mohair clean ever so carefully, never sparing the water. Then she spread the mohair on frames of wire mesh lying close to the ground. There the mohair would be drying in the sun while 'Mabonolo made fires under great big pots in which she was going to dye the mohair into many colours. When all the mohair had been dyed and dried, 'Mabonolo began to spin it into long strips of thread, colour by colour.

Then followed the part that Bonolo loved most: the time of silence. That was when all the wonderful things he could ever think of were made; when what was not there a few moments before, suddenly appeared, and was there. That was when 'Mabonolo sat at her desk in the rondavel, making elaborate designs on paper. Then she picked out a design and went over to the loom, where she began to weave tapestry.

Yes, it was at such moments that pictures of great beauty came out of her deft fingers: the mountain forests of Iketsetse; the rolling fields of corn, wheat and sorghum; tall aloes silhouetted against a rising moon; snow, turning fields and mountains into endless, rolling whiteness; eagles, kestrels, and bald-headed vultures soaring high above the clouds; horses and their riders making giant leaps over great gorges; people working in the fields; children playing hopscotch; women threshing wheat; men cutting down trees; people riding buses; people dancing merrily; mourners at funerals. What picture could 'Mabonolo not make on her tapestries? The entire history of the village of Iketsetse came out of her marvellous fingers.

Bonolo marvelled at it all, awed by what silence could do. That, he decided, would be his life: a life of silence, in which he would be free to create anything he wanted in the world. Then the inevitable happened! Just as Bonolo had felt that he had become a carpenter like his father, so he now felt that he had become a weaver, like his mother. In the same way, with his eyes closed, he began to make in his mind tapestries, the beauty of which had never been seen in the world.

Before long, 'Mabonolo began to worry about her son. She understood now what her husband had been saying to her all along. What kind of child was this who wanted nothing more than to sit all day, eyes closed, an enchanted look on his face? What kind of child was this who did not want to play with other children in the village, who did not even play alone? She must talk things over with her husband.

One night, when they thought Bonolo was asleep, Rabonolo and 'Mabonolo sat together, and, for a long time, asked themselves once again the same endless questions about their son. They were worried.

What kind of child was this who did not walk through the streets of the village seeing its buildings and meeting its people; who did not go out into the fields to watch the birds in the sky, and learn about hares, field mice, and lizards on the ground; who did not see flying insects in the sky, and crawling insects on the earth; who did not disappear like other boys into the surrounding mountains, there to wander through the forests that the people of Iketsetse had created with their own hands, generation after generation? What kind of child was this? And the people of Iketsetse, what did they think of such a boy? What worth would he be to his community?

As Rabonolo and 'Mabonolo were busy asking themselves questions and trying to answer them, they did not know that Bonolo was not asleep;

22

that their questions and answers were giving him ideas he was to use in the next few months. Strangely enough, as he listened to his parents, Bonolo realised he was himself far from happy with his life. Surely there was something more in the world than carpentry and weaving!

So far, his dream world had not gone beyond furniture and tapestry. Indeed, his mind was filled only with furniture and tapestry. Whatever he saw, he turned into furniture and tapestry, like that king of ancient times who turned everything he touched into gold. There was furniture and tapestry everywhere: furniture and tapestry in the sky; furniture and tapestry on the earth. He was growing tired of furniture and tapestry. It was then that he began to be terrified of his own thoughts, for even the very food he ate turned into furniture and tapestry.

And so it happened that when Rabonolo and 'Mabonolo finally went to bed, still worried and without any answers, their son closed his eyes, a smile on his face, and fell asleep.

The following day 'Mabonolo went to her rondavel as usual. And, as usual, she expected her son to come in and sit on the mat next to her. In fact, to 'Mabonolo, who had become so used to the presence of her son, Bonolo had become part of the rondavel, like the spinning-wheel, the loom, and the threads. If one day she were to come into the rondavel to work and not find the spinning-wheel in there, she would definitely say: 'Where is my spinning-wheel?' If the loom were missing, she would say: 'Where is my loom?' As the sun rose higher and higher, and Bonolo did not come in as usual to take his place on the floor, 'Mabonolo asked: 'Where is my son?'

Because she missed her son, 'Mabonolo stood up, went to the door, and called out to him. There was no answer.

She went back to her loom. But once there, she found she could not concentrate. She walked out of the rondavel to the house, where she searched in each and every room. No sign of Bonolo. Then she went outside and cast her eyes towards the carpentry shop from where she could hear the sound of hammering. She wondered if Bonolo was there. She called out again. Still no answer.

Of course she should go to the workshop, thought 'Mabonolo. How foolish she had been! Clearly, with all the hammering in there, Bonolo would not be able to hear his mother's call. But there was no sign of Bonolo in the workshop.

'Is he not with you?' asked Rabonolo.

'No,' replied 'Mabonolo. 'And I have looked everywhere in the house.'

'That is strange,' said Rabonolo, rolling with his fingers the pencil behind his ear. He always did that when he was puzzled or thinking hard. Finally he said: 'You go to the Pulas on the left; I'll go the Nalas on the right.'

5

Where Is Bonolo?

NONE OF the neighbours had seen Bonolo, and Rabonolo and 'Mabonolo began to worry. How could their child disappear under their very eyes? They had to look for him.

'Have you seen Bonolo?' they asked people in the streets.

'No,' some said, and then went on to ask: 'Has anything happened to him?'

Rabonolo and 'Mabonolo would explain, and the people said, 'We will keep our eyes open for him.'

'Have you seen Bonolo?' Rabonolo and 'Mabonolo asked yet another lot of people.

'Who is that?'

'Our son.'

'Oh, pardon us, we had forgotten that you had a son. He must have grown into a little man to be getting lost now.'

Rabonolo and 'Mabonolo felt sad that there were some people in the village who did not know Bonolo. It was not right. A person must be known to his community.

Before long, the alarm had spread, and the whole village was looking for Bonolo. At last he was found at the village stables, lying on his back against a little hill of hay, gazing at horses.

'Bonolo!' said the men who found him. 'You have given your parents and everyone such a fright. What are you doing here?'

Bonolo stared at them as if he did not see them. Indeed, he did not see them. The look on his face was that of someone to whom the world around did not exist. He was deep in his thoughts. It took his father to shake Bonolo out of his trance.

'What is it you're doing here?' Rabonolo asked his son.

'Horse-racing, father,' said Bonolo calmly. All the searchers looked at one another and laughed, some shaking their heads.

Rabonolo and 'Mabonolo looked at each other, understanding what was happening.

The following day Bonolo disappeared again. Another alarm was raised. This time he was found on the roof of the market-place, gazing at all the activity below.

On yet another occasion he was found behind the altar of a church. Then he was found in the court house. And then again he was found in the dispensary at the hospital. Once he was found at the end of the airstrip where planes from Maseru landed and took off. In the end it was decided that everyone should be on the look-out for him. It became common in Iketsetse to see people now and again taking a peep around corners. A stranger would have been puzzled by all this.

Then Bonolo decided to take to the fields and the forests where he would not be found so easily by any prying search party. But even there things did not work out exactly according to his wishes.

Once he was found hiding in a bush where all day he had been watching the herd boys playing and talking and herding. Then again he was found eventually after a long day's search, sitting under a peach tree, his back against the trunk of the tree.

'And now,' the search party asked, 'what are you doing here to-day?'

Bonolo stared at them, not really seeing them, for he had been in a deep trance since early in the morning when he had disappeared from home and had found the peach tree in the fields.

The men of the search party gathered in a semi-circle around Bonolo, shutting him off from the hot rays of the afternoon sun. The resulting sudden, slight chill made Bonolo shiver for a fleeting moment, making him raise his knees. Then he put his arms around his knees, as if to turn himself into a ball so that he could keep warm.

Luckily for the search party, the little chill also

did something else: it seemed to rouse Bonolo from his trance somewhat. He began to speak, and the men, who had been talking among themselves in low, concerned voices, trying to discuss what to do about Bonolo, hushed and listened.

'I can hear a deep rumble of heavy voices,' began Bonolo. 'I can't hear exactly what they are saying. Sometimes they sound like the groans of people in pain at the hospital; sometimes they sound like the moans of sad people, mourning at a funeral service in church; sometimes they sound like the roar of an aeroplane landing or taking off at the airport.'

The men looked at one another, still wondering what to do. At that point Bonolo seemed to come out fully from his trance, and carried on his face the look of someone who had just come back from a long, long journey. He looked at the men, smiled, and spoke again:

'The world is beautiful,' he said. 'Look at all the furniture I have made. Look at the tapestry I have made: rolling fields upon rolling fields of it, so that there is no grass any more in the world. It has all turned into tapestry.

'Look. I have filled every stall in the marketplace with fruits and vegetables. I have raised horses that can win every race. And the hospitals. Look at them: they are empty. I have cured everyone and rid the world of pain and disease.

'And the churches? Let all people put their prayer books away, for I have made everyone holy. Isn't the world wonderful? And now, fathers, leave me, for I have a lot of work to do.'

The men looked at one another again, and exchanged meaningful glances. This time, though, they nodded at one another. Without exchanging a word, they picked up Bonolo and carried him home.

6

The Peach Tree

THAT NIGHT Rabonolo and 'Mabonolo sat down to talk about their son once more. Although they were worried about him, wondering what would become of him, they decided to leave him alone. Perhaps, sooner or later, they hoped, the boy would outgrow his strange ways. What use was there in prodding an ant back to its colony? Better let it go. Sooner or later it would find its way home. Where did this ant go? Back to that peach tree in the fields where it would sit all day, shifting its position around the tree because the sun called out to be followed. That tree, the ant decided, would be its home. There was no point any more in hiding.

In this way, the peach tree became Bonolo's place of work. It was now accepted in the village that Bonolo would get up in the morning like everybody else, have his breakfast, and then go to the fields where he would sit all day under his peach tree, his eyes closed, and his face turned towards the sun. And at the end of the day, as the sun went down, Bonolo would be seen returning home like all the other villagers, having done his day's work of dreaming.

Soon Bonolo found his way into the language of the village. At school, teachers often warned the children: 'No one who basks in Bonolo's sun will pass.' This was because in the village, people who sat lazily in the sun the whole day were said to be 'basking in Bonolo's sun'. Sometimes people, particularly children, found it difficult to leave the warmth of their blankets in the morning. They spent time musing and thinking about all kinds of pleasant things, making it even more difficult for themselves to get up. Then they were said to be 'having Bonolo's dreams'. Even patients at the hospital, who had been anaesthetized for operations, joked among themselves that they had been 'sent into Bonolo's world'.

Bonolo became Iketsetse's biggest curiosity. People in nearby villages came to know about him. Soon news of Bonolo spread far beyond Iketsetse. After Radio Lesotho had given a new report on him, he came to be known not only in the whole of Lesotho, but also in countries beyond. Visitors began to pour into Iketsetse to see for themselves this boy of strange and unusual ways.

The people of Iketsetse were uneasy at the sudden fame of their village as a result of Bonolo.

What example was this child going to be to other children, not only in Iketsetse, but also in the whole of Lesotho? If someone could be famous for sitting under a tree, dreaming, then soon every child would be looking for a tree to sit under and dream. And there were plenty of trees! The surrounding forests of Iketsetse would swallow up all their children. That is how it came to be that much was said to discourage behavior such as Bonolo's. This would be done at schools during morning assembly, and in sermons at church, and at village pitsos.

Much as they feared the possible influence of Bonolo's behaviour, the people of Iketsetse still worried about Bonolo. After all, he was one of the children of the village, a son to all, a brother to all. It was agreed that everyone was to help his parents keep an eye on him at all times to make sure he was safe. People who went out into the fields, to work there or to gather wood, were asked to pass by Bonolo's tree. Herd boys were particularly warned to watch him. Very often, though, people went out of their way not really to check on Bonolo, but to listen to him telling his fantastic stories.

'Bonolo,' said a man one morning, 'come and fish with me.' He was carrying fishing gear over his shoulder, and was on his way to fish at the Senqu river.

'Why do you trouble yourself so much, every day of your life?' asked Bonolo. 'I can help you get all the fish you need in the world.' And, as soon as he said so, he closed his eyes, and gathering his blanket around him, turned his face towards the morning sun, and continued: 'Sir, travel east all the way until you reach the village of Bochabelo. Once there, you should wait like all the villagers, to put your request before Naledi, the girl of the stars, whose beauty and age have remained unchanged beyond memory. She comes out only on the night of the full moon for people of her village to gaze at her beauty. They approach her also to receive all their wishes.

'Men who return from the mines with shattered legs come to her and say: "Naledi, please give me back my legs." And before you have blinked your eyes, they are up, walking away.

'And so too do the sick; and those who want their horses to win the races; and those who want to know what the future holds for them. Naledi, of endless youth, can also chase the drought away and bring plenty to the land.

'When your turn comes, deliver an urgent message from Bonolo. Tell her that the rivers of Iketsetse have dried up and all the fish have perished. She will say to you: "At the next full moon, go to the bank of the dry river, and look at the stars, and let the clear night carry your voice to me."

'"Naledi," you should say, "please fill the Senqu river with water." And the river will begin to flow. And then again you should say, "Naledi, please fill the water with fish." And then you will see in the moonlit sky a wonder you have never thought possible in the world. Countless stars will begin to fall in so many brilliant strips of light from the sky into the river. And once there each star will turn into a fish. And thereafter, for as long as there are stars in the sky, there will be plentiful fish in the Senqu river to feed people for many years to come. Now, Sir, if you really want fish, begin your journey to the east.'

The fisherman, in spite of himself, looked longingly in the direction of the east. But quickly he came to his senses, shook his head, and walked on towards the river. As he sat on the bank of the river, holding his fishing line, he did not feel lonely that day, and never came to know just how it was that he carried home five big fish at the end of the day.

One afternoon an old woman carrying a bundle of fire-wood on her head passed by Bonolo's tree and found him there sitting under the peach tree. 'My child,' she said, 'other boys are herding their fathers' cattle, sheep, and goats. Where are yours?'

Bonolo closed his eyes, turned his face towards the setting sun and said: 'There are my cattle, sheep and goats. Look at them. Look. The pasture is green and wet, and they have been eating and drinking all at once all day long. Now, their stomachs are full. They can hardly walk. What need do they have of me? Now, they are on their way home. It's all very easy. Just look at them.'

The old woman, turning her whole body, looked around, and saw nothing but dry yellow corn stalks rattling in the quiet afternoon breeze. She smiled and walked away home.

Sometimes, at midday, after they had hunted and roasted field rats for their midday meal, the herd boys would come to Bonolo's tree. They would listen to him telling them of all kinds of wonderful worlds wherein people just sat and things happened.

'Look at my peach tree,' Bonolo would say. 'Come spring, there will be wonderful pink blossoms. And, as sure as the sun will rise and set, there will be bees buzzing around from blossom to blossom. All the pollen in the world will be there for them, waiting for them. All the bees have to do is wait for spring. It's all very easy.' And Bonolo would tighten his closed eyes and see the ease and beauty of it all.

'Come summer,' he began again, 'the blossoms will be gone, having turned into beautiful red peaches, hidden away among thick, heavy green leaves. And the bees will be gone, leaving the tree to sparrows and me. Soon it will be the time of the peach juice. Far more pleasurable than the eating of the peach is the licking of peach juice around the lips or on the fingers. Especially between the fingers! Always leave, somewhere on the hand, a little patch of juice to dry until it turns sticky, for there is nothing more pleasurable than licking off the stickiness. And such is the joy of sitting under a tree that has given you so many peaches and shade. It's all very easy.' And Bonolo would tighten his closed eyes and see more clearly the wonder of it all.

There followed a silence in which the listening boys seemed to be forming pictures of great beauty in their minds, fixing on each detail of the picture with the wonder of recognition. When their pictures were complete, a new one would be ready in Bonolo's mind, and the boys waited for it.

'Come autumn,' Bonolo continued, the distant smile on his face giving way to sadness, 'suddenly, as if they had never been there, all the peaches will be gone. No bees. No sparrows. Just silence, made worse by the noiseless soaring of vultures high up in the sky, as silent as the leaves, now yellow, falling off the tree. Some leaves will stay on, though, until they become crisply brown, rattling when the wind blows. And all the while I'll be there, there under the rain of leaves, under the bones of branches slowly letting through more of the sun's gaze. I'll be there as the sky opens up to me until it is so vast that I will want to fill it up with something. And so, I lie on my back on the cushion of leaves, and, closing my eyes, I see the skies of my mind as vast as the open skies. And I fill it up with all the pictures of spring and summer just gone by.'

Without being aware, all the boys had closed their eyes as if to see more clearly the pictures of the world that Bonolo drew for them. But now, Bonolo did not pause; the pictures of autumn immediately gave way to new pictures of winter.

'And then, come winter,' he said, arriving at the end of his dream, and closing his eyes so tightly that there were creases on his forehead, 'no bees. No birds. No peaches. No leaves. Just me. Just me and the bare branches of the tree stretching out into the sky to catch the heat of the sun for me. But I'll sit there, my eyes closed, and my face turned towards the sun. I'll sit there until I am one with the sun. And every evening I'm going to return to the village, carrying all the heat of the sun with me, so that the people of the village can come and warm themselves off me, and be safe from the cold winter nights.'

And so, in this way, in Bonolo's mind, days passed into weeks, weeks into months. Seasons came and went. Bonolo sat under his peach tree. He had come a long way from the world of weaving and carpentry.

7

Bonolo Goes to School

BONOLO'S PARENTS began to worry again because soon it would be time for Bonolo and his age-mates to start going to school. Would their son go to school? They worried. But, like all the parents of Iketsetse, they began to make preparations: buying a uniform for Bonolo; buying a snack box; a school bag; new shoes and socks; pencils and pencil sharpeners, erasers, rulers and exercise books. Thus prepared, the people of Iketsetse waited for the first day of school. This was a great day in the village of Iketsetse. Nobody went to work that day. It was a holiday. Fathers, mothers, sisters, brothers, uncles, aunts, grandfathers and grandmothers all accompanied the children to school.

Year after year, one of the most memorable events of the first day of school was how old people told stories of their first day at school, and everybody listened as if it were the very first time they had heard the stories.

Parents met the teachers of the children, and were shown all they needed to know about the school. They were shown the classrooms where their children were going to learn; they were shown all the books and other things that their children were going to use to help them learn how to read and write; and they were shown around the school yards, the vegetable fields and sports fields.

That was the day when everyone in the village talked about education, and dreamed about what they hoped the new school-goers would become when they finished school. How would they serve the village? Who did not marvel at the new world that was opening up for their children: the world of reading, of writing, and of counting? There would be so many other things to learn about too: the rivers of Lesotho, from which Basotho drank; the air people breathed; the soil that fed them with fruit and vegetables; all the living things that shared the world with people: animals, insects, plants, trees. And there were the other villages to learn about too; the towns and districts of Lesotho, and then about far and distant people, countries, and planets far out in the universe.

But two parents were not sharing in the joy of the village. They were sad, for on that first day of school, their son got up as usual and headed for his peach tree in the fields. Rabonolo and 'Mabonolo

followed him, hoping to persuade him to come with them to school.

'Bonolo, my son,' said Rabonolo when they got to the tree, 'you must come with us to school. Today all your age-mates are going to school. You cannot sit here day after day with no friends. It is time for you to learn at school how you are going to live with them for the whole of your life.'

Bonolo closed his eyes and turned his face towards the sun. 'Father and mother,' he said, 'here under my tree I have the whole world. Here under the tree, I am never alone. Here under the tree I have schools, market-places, hospitals, sports fields, forests, mountains, and more people than you have ever seen in your lives.'

As Rabonolo and 'Mabonolo listened to their son dreaming as ever, a great sadness fell upon them. Why did they have a son who was so different from others? Why couldn't he see how important it was to go to school? As Rabonolo asked himself such questions, he grew angry. If his son could not see for himself the importance of going to school, then he must be made to. In a fit of anger, Rabonolo reached out with his great carpenter's arm, seized Bonolo's hand, jerked him to his feet, and began to drag him by the hand to school.

'Mabonolo, following a short distance behind, was alarmed. She had not thought things would turn out this way. Occasionally she shouted:

'Bonolo's father, mind the child's arm! You will tear off the child's arm!' But Rabonolo was too angry to hear. He just dragged Bonolo on, increasing his pace until Bonolo, in order not to trip over and fall, began to trot behind his father. Some villagers who saw what was happening were aghast. They wondered what had gone wrong with Rabonolo, a man known for his kindness, patience and tolerance. What on earth had happened to make him treat his child this way?

As would be expected, Bonolo's first day at school meant nothing to him. His mind was never at school. It was back there under his peach tree in the fields. There was a constant daze on his face which showed he was not paying attention to anything going on in class. And that is how it was for the entire first week and the next. It was pointless. In the end, after many meetings between the principal, Bonolo's teacher and Bonolo's parents, it was decided to let Bonolo return to his tree. What was the use? Only his body was at school. His mind was away at his tree.

In this way Bonolo returned to his peach tree in the fields. There he found new herd boys, for those of his age had gone to school. Bonolo noted this change and, in spite of himself, felt some kind of longing for those familiar faces. But he brushed away that feeling. That is how Bonolo resumed his dreaming under the peach tree in the field.

Summer passed. Autumn came. And winter.

Then spring. And sure enough, the pink peach blossoms appeared. With each passing day, as the blossoms grew bigger and bigger, everything seemed the way Bonolo had expected. Nothing would change. Trust his world to behave exactly as expected! And he dreamed the most wondrous of worlds.

8

Something Goes Wrong

ONE DAY Bonolo thought he felt something strange. It seemed as if something was missing. What was it? He was not sure. He closed his eyes and tried to think of the world about him exactly as he had expected it. Everything seemed perfect. But when he opened his eyes, he felt once more that something was missing. But what it was, he could not be sure. He tried to brush aside this feeling. He was never one to allow himself to worry too much about things. His dream world took care of all problems. But this strange feeling persisted. Again, he closed his eyes, trying to dream away the discomfort. When he failed, he began to worry. Clearly, something was wrong. He could not remember ever feeling this way before. He was not quite in control of things.

With each failed effort of the imagination, Bonolo became increasingly desperate. It's like when

45

you know something very well, but you fail to remember it just at the time when you need to. You'll not be at peace with yourself until you remember it. How can memory let you down like this? So it was with Bonolo. And because he could not do what he used to, his imagination began to slow down. It would continue to slow down until he found out why he was so uneasy. For someone who lived only to dream, surely the end of his dreaming would be the end of his life. Yet, the more he worried, the more the world in his mind became empty of images.

As he sat worrying he heard a distant drone in the sky. He was pleased to recognise it instantly. It was the plane from Maseru coming to land at Mokhotlong Airport. Indeed, well after he had recognised it in his mind, the plane passed over him, flying low as it prepared to land. Then it disappeared from view. Bonolo knew when it had landed from the lower sound it made as it taxied on the runway. Then a deep silence followed the cutting of the engines. Strange, thought Bonolo. A few minutes ago the roar of the aircraft had filled the sky; now, silence filled the sky. It was as if both sound and silence were things you could pick up with your hands and move from place to place!

And that was when he remembered, for just at that moment of deep silence, he heard a much softer drone, the kind of drone he had always expected in his mind at that time of the year. For that drone always ran through his body like a breeze, tickling his nerves.

That drone made it the only time of the year when he really felt the presence of his body. It was the drone of the bees. It sent a pleasant feeling down his spine, filling his entire body with a low, lulling, tingling sensation that brought him a feeling of unimaginable calm. That was the time his mind rested, thinking no thoughts, dreaming no dreams, as if it too were being prepared for the summer's harvest of fruity dreams.

Bonolo was pleased that he had remembered. He had remebered one of the most pleasant moments of his life under the tree. How obvious it all was! How on earth could he have forgotten? His faith in the powers of his imagination returned. But his joy was short-lived. It was only the joy of memory, for, otherwise, things were disturbingly not quite the same. Bonolo looked around and discovered that the customary drone was very weak. There was only a bee here, and another bee there, and that was all. There was none of the constant heavy buzz he knew so well; a buzz so heavy that when the tree's leaves were fully grown, hiding from view the hundreds of visiting bees, you might think the tree itself was buzzing; you might think the green colour of the leaves had turned into sound.

The following day was no different. There were no bees. Yet Bonolo continued to hope. The next day was no different. There were still no bees. Disturbed, Bonolo began to accept the fact that this spring no bees would visit his tree. But why? He could find no answer until a few days later, when upon a whim, he looked closely at his tree and discovered something terrifying. The pink blossoms of his peach tree were dying. They were slowly withering, turning limp, and their pink colour was fading into something like grey. Then they turned into a shining, filthy-looking black.

Was this something that affected his tree only? Bonolo stood up and cast his eyes around the valley. The valley was awash with the pink of peach blossoms. Here and there were spots of white where the apricot blossoms shone in the clear humid spring sun. What splendour!

Instead of feeling the soothing buzzing of the bees coursing through his body, Bonolo felt a violent tremor of terror shaking his body. He turned round to look at his tree, wishing, for the first time in his life, that what he was seeing was a mere dream. It was no dream. He saw dying and dead blossoms. Desperately he shut his eyes, and, with his mind, attempted to command the leaves to shoot out and cover the unbearable ugliness before him. Indeed, the leaves were not going to let him down. In a few days, they began to appear. There they were. He noted with satisfaction the same rich and thick green leaves that he had expected. But this was not to last.

After a while, the leaves themselves began to shrivel, turning into a sickly yellow. When this happened, Bonolo, once again, did an unusual thing. He stood up not only to examine his tree carefully, but also to touch its blossoms.

'Disgusting!' he thought, withdrawing his hand as if from a flame. Although he had not touched many things in his life, not even the healthy pink blossoms of last year, he knew that the feel of the dying blossoms was unpleasant. Now all black and shiny, the blossoms felt slimy, just like one of the few things he had to touch, especially in winter when he had to wipe it off his face: mucus.

Then he looked at the leaves. He had never really touched them either. All he had known were the yellow leaves of autumn which fell on him on their own. Many would be left to dry on the tree. These too were shaken down on him by the winds. But now, as he looked at the fresh leaves dying, he felt a deep need to touch them, not just for the sake of touching them, but because he felt somehow that touching them might have something to do with helping his tree. He touched them. The leaves were also sticky, so sticky that if he did not pull away his finger quickly, he thought he might be glued to the tree forever.

Looking at his fingers after lifting them off the leaves, he noticed something that made his whole body shudder with terror; there were tiny green creatures on his fingers. Desperately, he shook them off, and looked closely at the leaves again. He saw that the tiny green creatures, aphids, were all over the tree, on each and every leaf. But that was not all. He realised also that something like the glue in his father's carpentry workshop was oozing out of the trunk of the tree. Supposing he touched *that?* Would

he be glued to the tree forever? The more he thought about it, the more terrified he became. But still the thought gripped him. The uncertainty tugged at him violently. Yes, supposing he touched that glue? His mind began to be invaded by the horror of it all.

Helplessly he felt his imagination running away from him like a bird which flies away just out of reach when you want to catch it. Bonolo could not stop his mind running on its own. He had trained it well. It could think of anything. But he had never expected it to bring so much pain and suffering to him.

Clearly, in Bonolo's mind, the sweet juice of ripe peaches, that juice that he had imagined so many times, had suddenly turned into the slimy liquid of rotting peach blossoms. He felt as if it were dripping down onto his body, slowly covering him. The tiny green creatures turned into gigantic bees feeding on the slime on him. Soon enough they would finish the slime and begin to feed on him!

9
Bonolo's Agony

AS SURELY as his mind worked, Bonolo began to feel as if he were himself turning into his rotting tree, and the glue that oozed out of the tree now came out of gigantic sores all over his body. And the glue turned into pus. And what a stench there was around the tree!

In desperation, Bonolo tried to run away from his imagination. He sat down again and closed his eyes. He turned his face towards the sun, hoping to bring back once more into his mind, a beautiful world. After all, hadn't the tree become a part of him? He could turn its branches into fields of corn. He could turn its leaves into beautiful snowflakes, or sorghum seeds, or into sods that he could break when he ploughed the soil of his mind to plant seeds in its endless fields. He could dream of endless harvests, feeding all the people in the world. Yes, he could even mould the stem of the tree into a house, and build as many villages as people in the world wanted. All these dreams Bonolo tried to bring back now. But it was in vain.

When he closed his eyes, the ugliness of his tree simply grew more menacing. When he opened them, he would see the tree, less ugly than the tree in his mind, but definitely ugly. Its new branches dried up into lifeless twigs that fell off. Its trunk rotted away, seeming to emit a terrible smell, and dripped with what in Bonolo's mind had formed into pus. Try as he might to think of the most beautiful tree in the world, his dying peach tree remained fixed in his imagination like an ink-stain that could never be removed. It stood there foul-smelling and dripping.

And so Bonolo began to live in a world of unimaginable terror. He began to be afraid of sleep. How could he risk closing his eyes? He feared even to blink! Now that he feared what used to bring him so much pleasure, he shuddered at the thought of having to close his eyes and bring back the possibility of dreaming again. But night had to come. In the darkness Bonolo did not need to close his eyes to turn on his imagination. He saw the ugly world of his tree with his eyes open. He could conquer the darkness only by closing his eyes and bringing back with his mind the light of the day. But he would not close his eyes for fear of sleeping and thus leaving himself to the mercy of sleep's uncontrollable nightmares. Oh, what could he do?

Hours passed into days, and days passed into
weeks. Bonolo could not sleep. And the more he
stayed awake, the uglier his tree became. It became a
monster of towering proportions. Pus and slime
flowed from it, and soon there was nothing to drink in
the world but pus and slime. The air became foul with
the stench. All things, following Bonolo's tree, began
to die. All things were trapped in pus and slime that
had caked under the heat of a merciless sun.
Everything. What else was there to eat? What else was
there to drink? There was nothing left but the end of
all things.

    'What can I do to save my tree?' Bonolo
asked himself.

For the first time in his life, Bonolo realised that his imagination could not help him. He wanted to run away from all his thoughts now. But how could he? He had become his dreams. He had turned his life into an endless nightmare. What was worse, he could not turn to anyone for help. He did not know how to ask for help. He had run away from learning how to help in the carpentry shop. He had refused all offers of help from his mother and father. He had turned his friend away. Nor could he get help from anybody else in the village. Here was a boy who did not even know who his relatives were.

Rabonolo and 'Mabonolo began to notice that there was something wrong with their son. He was not eating. He was not drinking anything. How could he? They noticed also that their son looked endlessly tired. His eyes were red and drooping. Rabonolo and 'Mabonolo determined to find out what was wrong with their son.

'What is wrong, Bonolo?' they would ask.

But their son would merely stare back at them. Meanwhile, as they waited for him to say something, Bonolo would gradually see them turn into his monstrous tree. And he would cringe from them and scream in terror. Desperately needing to do something for her son, 'Mabonolo reached out to embrace him, as if her caring arms could clear away all his suffering. It was then that she felt, seeping through her dress into her breasts, the heat of fever in his body. She clung to her son all the more. Bonolo's screams and struggles to break free became as frenzied as his mother's efforts to offer him comfort and protection.

'Save me! Save me!' screamed Bonolo, writhing and wriggling like a little chick in its final struggle to break free out of the eggshell that was its home until it was time to be born. 'The tree! The tree has got me!' He screamed until the noise and his struggles became unbearable, and 'Mabonolo was forced to let him go. She watched him fly to a corner and saw him squeeze himself into it as if he wished to be swallowed up by it.

How could the pain in 'Mabonolo's face be described? To be rejected by what she loved most in the world! As they looked helplessly at their son huddled in the corner, Rabonolo and 'Mabonolo began to puzzle out something in their minds. The tree? What tree? The peach tree? How had it 'got' him? What was the meaning of their son's words?

One morning, Rabonolo and 'Mabonolo noticed that their son did not get up to go to his tree as usual. In any case, having discovered his fever, they had decided not to allow him to leave the house until he was better, even if it meant chaining the boy to his bed. But they found him in bed, awake and staring at the ceiling, wet with the sweat of fever. He saw them and immediately they noticed something remarkable. Bonolo's eyes began to blink rapidly and then he would hold them open as if he wished never to blink again. How could they know what was happening in their son's mind?

As soon as Bonolo saw them, his mind, as usual, began to turn them into monstrous trees, but this time he tried to fight off the transformation. He was struggling in his mind like one who is caught in a long terrible dream, and, ensnared between waking and sleeping, is aware that he is dreaming, and is struggling to awake. Finally, after what seemed an endless struggle, he opened his eyes to the freedom and relief of wakefulness. Bonolo fought off the nightmare as if that were the most vital thing in his life at that time. And he spoke: 'Father and mother,' he said, struggling to say the words. 'My tree. It is dying.' That is all he said. All he had been striving to say. Then he closed his eyes and began a long, dreamless sleep.

It was sleep of the deepest kind. Bonolo was sent into a world of vast darkness where there was only silence and stillness. It was the kind of silence and stillness he had enjoyed in his waking moments when, with his eyes closed, he wondered what his mother or father were creating out of their drawings. How did things come out of silence? How did they come out of the darkness behind his eyes? The longer the silence, the longer would be the darkness. The longer the silence and darkness, the greater the freshness and enchantment of what would be created. That was what Bonolo experienced when he was awake and imagining things. But now, in his deep sleep, was he himself being made in the silence and darkness of his sleep? When he opened his eyes finally, what kind of world would have been created before him?

10

The Village Helps

WHEN BONOLO finally came out of his long
sleep, he opened his eyes to a room full of
people. He saw his parents; he recognised some of the
people who used to stop by at his tree for a story or
two; he saw some of the age-mates he had seen in the
fields but whose names he did not know, and who had
since gone to school. He saw teachers, priests, farmers,
other village carpenters and weavers, bus drivers,
market sellers, electricians, shop owners, doctors,
nurses, footballers, musicians. Many of these people
had come to his home to collect furniture they had
ordered. Who was not there in his house to see him
return to the world?

As soon as word had spread in the village that
Bonolo was seriously ill, people had come in and out
of Bonolo's home to comfort and help his parents
nurse him back to health. Many were there when he

opened his eyes, and as he looked at all those people around his bed, it was as if he were seeing people for the first time in his life. And, without being aware of what he was doing, he reached out with his hands, wanting to touch all of them. They came in turns to shake his hand.

How different each hand was! Some were soft, some hard, some warm, some cold, some dry, and some wet. So many hands! Different hands doing different kinds of work. What different things did they handle and bring together in all kinds of ways to make new things? It was as if Bonolo, through those hands, and for the first time in his life, felt the world of real things: things to touch and then know. He was to remember, for a long time after, the feel of each and every hand he shook that day.

His friend, Tsepo, was there too. He stood next to the bed, looking at Bonolo as if he were ready to ask him once more to come along on a bus ride.

A few days later, when he got out of bed, with his friend next to him and helping him along, Bonolo wanted to do nothing more than touch everything he came across. The world was new. What was it he wanted to do? He wanted to make all those things his age-mates used to make in the fields as he sat motionless under his peach tree.

There were all those cars and buses he wanted to make with wire. He wished to get himself cut too, and see his own blood, and taste it too, the way he used to see the other boys sucking their bleeding

61

fingers. There was all that animal life to cast in clay dug from the banks of the Senqu river. Especially the great bulls! How would he fare in the competitions to find out who made the best bull in clay? And those fine fighting sticks? He wanted to make them too. What of all the village trades? Overwhelmed by all the questions he asked himself, Bonolo looked at his hands and knew how ignorant they were of the real things of the world.

And so it was, that although there was only one week of school left, Bonolo started going to school, determined to learn as much as he could. Never had a child so wanted to go to school! His parents' joy was too great to be described. But it was too late. Too late. Bonolo could never learn enough to be ready for that other great day in the village of Iketsetse: the very last day of school.

On the day, mothers and fathers, sisters, brothers, uncles and aunts, grandmothers and grandfathers, the mayoress of Iketsetse, the postmistress, doctors and nurses at the hospital, the village priests, the chief of police, and other important elected officials of the village, famous workers, craftsmen and craftswomen, musicians, actors, and sports personalities all visited the village schools. They wanted to see what the children of Iketsetse had done during the whole year of learning.

Try as he might, Bonolo could never learn how to write in a week; not when he was still struggling just to hold a pencil. Try as he might, he could never learn in a week the secrets of numbers and the joy of counting up to one hundred. How could he master the alphabet and recognise all those letters brought together to form words; how could he learn to prepare a vegetable plot and learn the names of all the vegetables he would need to plant? When would he learn all the names of rivers, mountains, animals, insects, trees and other things about the world that are so important? Not in a week.

The great day came. How Bonolo wished it wouldn't. But it had to. Like the seasons that governed the life of his peach tree, the day could never be put off. For the whole week the schools prepared for it as they had done for many years. All the more then, Bonolo could not learn much that week. Preparations for the great day took away all the time. All the work of the children was arranged according to the different subjects under the names of the children. And Bonolo? It was decided that he too would have to display the fruits of his work.

First, there was a table with insect collections: but there was nothing under the name of Bonolo. Next were the samples of leaves of different trees: but there was nothing under the name of Bonolo. Then there were the samples of arts and crafts: drawings of different birds, paintings of many colours, models of the village, knitted work, and several other things. Still, there was nothing under the name of Bonolo. Outside, there were neat green patches of garden plots with different kinds of vegetables that the

children had planted and tended. Although Bonolo had not attended school, he had also been given a plot. It bore his name, but it was so full of weeds that the other children had learned about the different kinds of weeds from that plot.

As the other children took their parents round explaining to them what they had learned, all Bonolo could say to his parents, as he walked with them from table to table, was: 'I have done nothing!' As he continued to see the work of other children, the pain of not having anything to show became unbearable, and Bonolo broke down and cried.

Everybody saw those tears coming out of those famous eyes which were known to see more clearly

when they were closed. How could people forget the wonderful visions they had been made to see? The tears were a message: something had to be done to help this child of Iketsetse. It was decided.

The schools were closed for the Christmas holidays. But it would be no holiday for Bonolo and his age-mates. While his teacher helped him to read and write and count, his age-mates volunteered to help him gather insects. They taught him the names of trees and rivers and the mountains of Lesotho.

This pupil never tired of asking questions. He would be seen all over the village asking people what work they were doing. And everyone would patiently explain things to him, for at Iketsetse, knowledge was given to whoever wanted it. Often Bonolo was invited to help so that he could learn by doing. Driven on by his hunger to learn, he learned much very quickly. Now he could be sent alone to the shops, for he knew how to count money. He learned how to make some joints in his father's carpentry shop. He drew patterns for his mother's tapestry. He had his own garden plot at home where he saw the vegetable seeds he had sown rise into plants. And he marvelled at the pleasing coarseness of soil in his hands, and the freshness of its smell. There were so many things to do!

11

The Feast and the Dream

OF ALL the things in the world Bonolo wanted
to do, there was one that he desperately wanted
more than others. But he could not face the thought
of it. He was afraid even to express a wish, lest all the
terrible pains of the past returned. He went to all the
corners of Iketsetse, but never to that one spot that he
really wanted to see. Yet he knew that he would never
really be happy unless he went back there. His tree!
What was it like now? Would it still be shrivelled up,
dead? Should he go back there to see what had just
recently given him so much pain and suffering? How
could he abandon it now when it surely needed him
most? Hadn't he been helped by the whole village
when they could so easily have thrown him off? He
would need to gather enough courage to approach
his father about this matter. It was while Bonolo was
agonising that something happened.

Bonolo's parents decided to hold a feast to celebrate their son's return to health, and to thank the community for its support during difficult times. What a big feast it was! Almost all the villagers were there. There were swarms of children! Never had Bonolo seen so much dancing. The men wore black trousers, white long-sleeved shirts, black socks and white socks. They had silver armbands on their upper arms with handkerchiefs tucked into the armbands in such a way that they hung loosely down the arm, wafting this way and that during the dance. More handkerchiefs dangled from each side pocket of the men's trousers. The men were singing and dancing to the rhythm of an accordion and drums. Each man held a stick in one hand while a blanket hung loosely over the other shoulder.

There were women dancers too! They wore colourful dresses with rims of petticoats underneath. Whenever they walked the dresses swished to and fro like waves in the sea. When they sat down on their haunches to dance the *mokhibo,* their dresses flared around them in a mound of cloth, as if they sat on cushions of petticoats. Then, to the utmost pleasure of the guests, the dancers got up to their feet at the end of the dance to deliberately swish their dresses this way and that in a flurry of movement.

Children chased one another excitedly, often colliding into their parents. 'Go play far from here!' shouted the adults who had been bumped into. Sometimes they realised that the offender was none other than Bonolo himself, and an apology would follow. 'We didn't realise it was you, our great king. We are here because of you,' they would say, laughing. But the king, not hearing the apology, would be off again in pursuit of one of his subjects through a forest of adults, his little feet raising small squirts of dust which disappeared into the clouds of dust made by the armbanded dancers. Oh, what joy!

That night, tired in his bed, Bonolo closed his eyes, went into a deep sleep and had a dream. He saw multitudes of people in an endless, desolate orchard of dead peach trees. Around each tree was a group of people turning the soil at the base of the tree. Some were cutting dead branches off. Then there were chains of people passing buckets of water from person to person to water the trees. Soon the work was done. As the people stood back to see what they had done, something marvellous happened. New branches shot out of each tree, and blossoms followed, spreading a flame of pink throughout the orchard. The leaves unfurled, rounding out each tree like a green mushroom. The entire orchard, which only a few moments ago had been a desolate place, was now lush with green, shady peach trees.

Then all of a sudden, as if upon a signal, the trees wafted up into the sky like the silky seeds of a cottonwood tree. Their roots hung down like so many dangling large earthworms. The excited voices of people, who were being carried up with the trees, could be heard coming through the thick leaves as the

trees rose higher and higher. Soon the sky was filled
with floating trees that covered the earth far beyond
the horizon.

And then again, as if upon a signal, a rain of
peaches began to fall from the trees onto the earth, and
the people on the trees in the sky broke into a chorus of
celebration, filling the skies with songs of harvest. And
the rain of peaches continued without end. . . .

When Bonolo woke up the following morning, he felt inexplicably at peace with himself. He felt as if everything around him were new. He felt the urge to rise and see the fresh morning outside. Once there, he saw that his father, long up, was already in the garden working on the small circle of soil at the base of a tree. He was gently turning the soil. Bonolo shuddered with recognition. It was exactly what the people had been doing in his dream! Then he remembered that several times in the past he had seen his father turning the soil around the base of the trees in the garden, but he had never bothered to think further about it. Bonolo thought about his own tree and realised with relief that this time he felt no dread or fear. It seemed to him at that moment, that the future of his tree had some connection with his dream and what his father was doing in the garden.

In the days that followed, Bonolo began to tell stories again. Villagers would come to his place in the evenings to hear him weave his tales. Released from the horrors of his illness, his mind worked freely now. From now on he knew how to control his imagination so that he could tell stories not only of the utmost joy, but also of the deepest sadness.

Then one evening his father said to him: 'Son, we have all seen your tree. It can be saved. But it will need time, patience and a lot of work. My carpenter friends, the village fruit-tree growers and I put our heads together.' And as his father went on explaining, Bonolo remembered what his father had said once, that in Iketsetse, it was not enough simply to be a carpenter, one had to know everything there was to know about the world of trees from which all wood came. Meanwhile, his father would teach him how to tend his peach tree: how to prune the tree at the right time; how to apply manure and turn the soil around the base of the tree, and how to water it regularly with enough water to ensure that it bore juicy fruit.

In time, the tree regained its health. It bore some fruit the following year, but not much. And that first harvest was certainly not as delicious as the peaches of Bonolo's mind. Clearly, the tree was not yet itself. He had to wait for its full recovery. Until then, he would give it all the care in the world.

And so in the years that followed Bonolo knew, through the care that he lavished on his tree, that the dreams in his head would never add to anything if they did not tell his hands to make the world beautiful, and more beautiful, and more beautiful. Each year he looked after his tree with the greatest care; and each year it yielded the largest, the most delicious, and most beautiful peaches ever seen. His pride knew no bounds. What did he do with them? He never sold them: not a single peach. Every year, after picking the peaches, he would be seen going from house to house, leaving in each house a peach, the gift of his work, in appreciation for all the village had done for him.

Thus, once more, Bonolo enriched the language of the village. Everything that people valued highly, anything that had to be looked after carefully, to be cherished above all others, at all times, was called 'Bonolo's Tree'. For example, at important gatherings in the village, when people talked about how important the village of Iketsetse was to them, various speakers would be heard saying, 'This village is Bonolo's Tree. Let us love it and take care of it.' Or, when people expressed their thankfulness for having received a gift from others, they would say, 'Thank you! I will treasure this gift like Bonolo's Tree.'

Even more important, Bonolo never stopped telling stories. The villagers continued to gather at his home to listen to him tell the most beautiful stories. This time, the stories were richer than ever, because they were filled with things to touch, to smell, to taste, to hear, and to see, so that even in the wildest fantasy they saw the strength and beauty of truth. And when the people rose to return to their homes late at night, moved by Bonolo's latest story, they felt that the endless, silent sky above them was full of messages which they would spend their entire lives trying to find and understand. They were grateful for one thing: there was someone in the village who possessed the gift to help them find as many of those messages as was possible.

As they entered their yards they could hear Bonolo's voice, reaching out to them as if from the distant corners of the universe, telling them of the one reason for life: to ever know and to dream and to create; to make life beautiful.